1 PIANO, 4 HANDS

PIANO DUET PLAY-ALONG
VOLUME 45

AUDIO ACCESS INCLUDED

COLDPLAY

T0079170

PLAYBACK+
Speed • Pitch • Balance • Loop

To access audio visit:
www.halleonard.com/mylibrary

3688-3871-4438-6632

Photo by Ethan Miller/Getty Images

ISBN 978-1-4950-0893-1

HAL•LEONARD®
CORPORATION
7777 W. BLUEMOUND RD. P.O. BOX 13819 MILWAUKEE, WI 53213

Visit Hal Leonard Online at
www.halleonard.com

CONTENTS

CLOCKS

Words and Music by GUY BERRYMAN,
JON BUCKLAND, WILL CHAMPION
and CHRIS MARTIN

PARADISE

Words and Music by GUY BERRYMAN,
JON BUCKLAND, WILL CHAMPION,
CHRIS MARTIN and BRIAN ENO

15

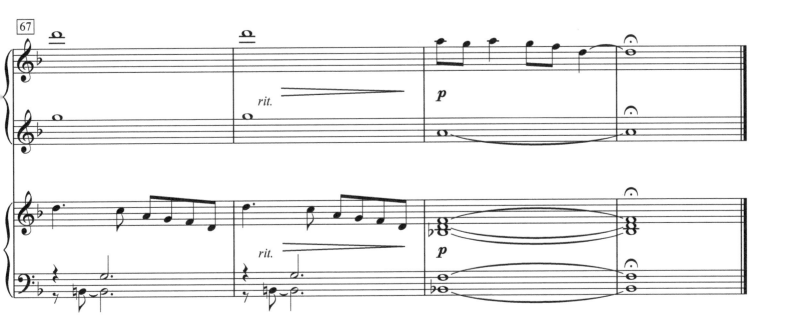

THE SCIENTIST

Words and Music by GUY BERRYMAN,
JON BUCKLAND, WILL CHAMPION
and CHRIS MARTIN

SPEED OF SOUND

Words and Music by GUY BERRYMAN,
JON BUCKLAND, WILL CHAMPION
and CHRIS MARTIN

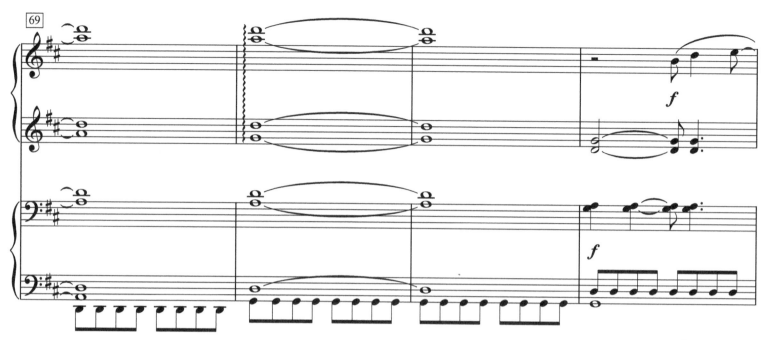

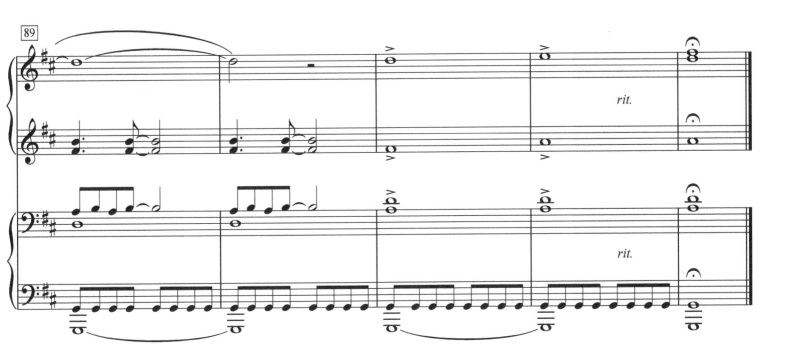

TROUBLE

Words and Music by GUY BERRYMAN,
JON BUCKLAND, WILL CHAMPION
and CHRIS MARTIN

CODA

VIVA LA VIDA

Words and Music by GUY BERRYMAN,
JON BUCKLAND, WILL CHAMPION
and CHRIS MARTIN

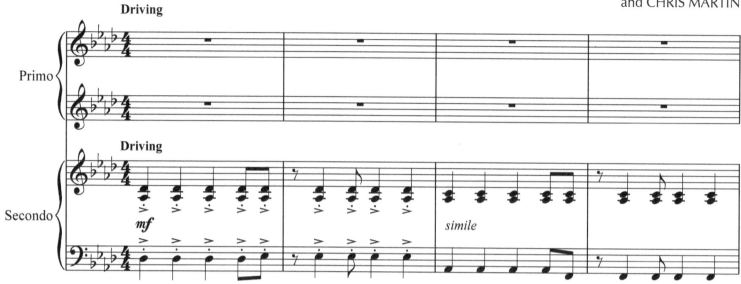

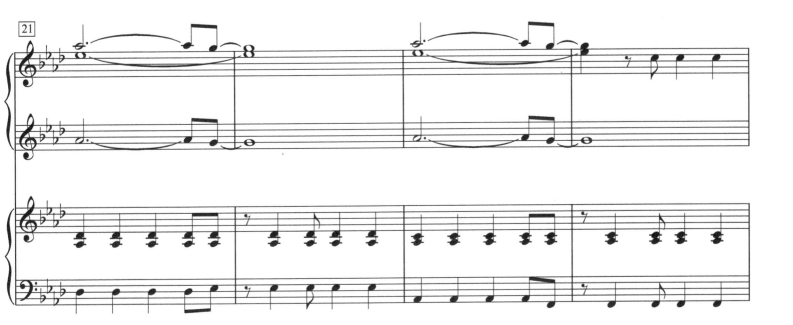

CODA

A SKY FULL OF STARS

Words and Music by GUY BERRYMAN,
JON BUCKLAND, WILL CHAMPION,
CHRIS MARTIN and TIM BERGLING

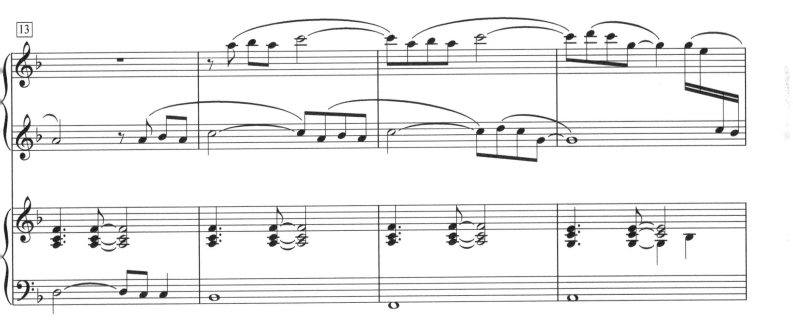

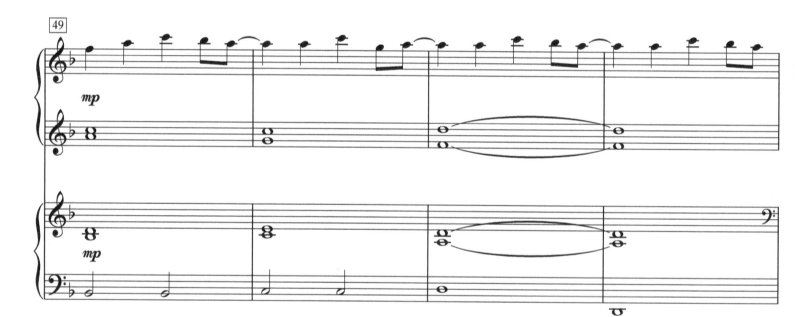

YELLOW

Words and Music by GUY BERRYMAN,
JON BUCKLAND, WILL CHAMPION
and CHRIS MARTIN

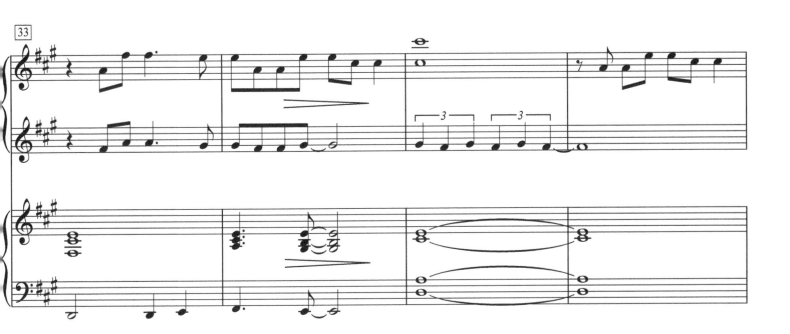

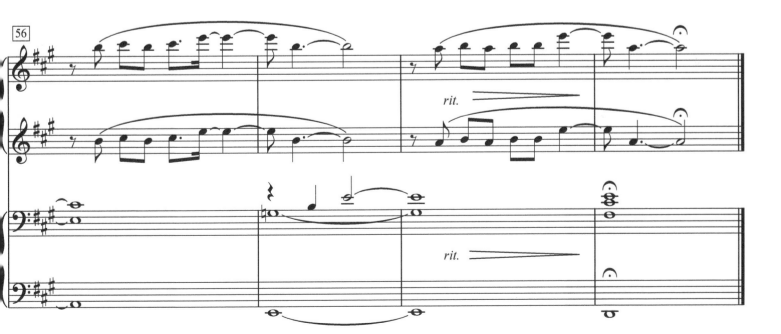

PIANO DUETS

The **Piano Duet Play-Along** series is an excellent source for 1 piano, 4 hand duets in every genre! It also gives you the flexibility to rehearse or perform piano duets anytime, anywhere! Play these delightful tunes with a partner, or use the accompanying audio to play along with either the Secondo or Primo part on your own. The audio files are enhanced so performers can adjust the recording to any tempo without changing pitch.

1. Piano Favorites
00290546 Book/CD Pack $14.95

2. Movie Favorites
00290547 Book/CD Pack $14.95

3. Broadway for Two
00290548 Book/CD Pack $14.95

4. The Music of Andrew Lloyd Webber™
00290549 Book/CD Pack $14.95

5. Disney Favorites
00290550 Book/CD Pack $14.95

6. Disney Songs
00290551 Book/CD Pack $14.95

7. Classical Music
00290552 Book/CD Pack $14.95

8. Christmas Classics
00290554 Book/CD Pack $14.95

9. Hymns
00290556 Book/CD Pack $14.95

10. The Sound of Music
00290557 Book/CD Pack $17.99

11. Disney Early Favorites
00290558 Book/CD Pack $16.95

12. Disney Movie Songs
00290559 Book/Online Audio $16.99

13. Movie Hits
00290560 Book/CD Pack $14.95

14. Les Misérables
00290561 Book/CD Pack $16.95

15. God Bless America® & Other Songs for a Better Nation
00290562 Book/CD Pack $14.99

16. Disney Classics
00290563 Book/CD Pack $16.95

19. Pirates of the Caribbean
00290566 Book/CD Pack $16.95

20. Wicked
00290567 Book/CD Pack $16.99

21. Peanuts®
00290568 Book/CD Pack $16.99

22. Rodgers & Hammerstein
00290569 Book/CD Pack $14.99

23. Cole Porter
00290570 Book/CD Pack $14.99

24. Christmas Carols
00290571 Book/CD Pack $14.95

25. Wedding Songs
00290572 Book/CD Pack $14.99

26. Love Songs
00290573 Book/CD Pack $14.99

27. Romantic Favorites
00290574 Book/CD Pack $14.99

28. Classical for Two
00290575 Book/CD Pack $14.99

29. Broadway Classics
00290576 Book/CD Pack $14.99

30. Jazz Standards
00290577 Book/CD Pack $14.99

31. Pride and Prejudice
00290578 Book/CD Pack $14.99

32. Sondheim for Two
00290579 Book/CD Pack $16.99

33. Twilight
00290580 Book/CD Pack $14.99

36. Holiday Favorites
00290583 Book/CD Pack $14.99

37. Christmas for Two
00290584 Book/CD Pack $14.99

38. Lennon & McCartney Favorites
00290585 Book/CD Pack $14.99

39. Lennon & McCartney Hits
00290586 Book/CD Pack $14.99

40. Classical Themes
00290588 Book/Online Audio $14.99

41. The Phantom of the Opera
00290589 Book/CD Pack $16.99

42. Glee
00290590 Book/CD Pack $16.99

43. A Merry Little Christmas
00102044 Book/CD Pack $14.99

44. Frozen
00128260 Book/Online Audio $14.99

45. Coldplay
00141054 Book/Online Audio $14.99

View complete songlists at
Hal Leonard Online at **www.halleonard.com**

Disney characters and artwork are © Disney Enterprises, Inc.